**COUNTRIES**

# ETHIOPIA

by Samantha S. Bell

FOCUS READERS®
NAVIGATOR

WWW.FOCUSREADERS.COM

Copyright © 2025 by Focus Readers®, Mendota Heights, MN 55120. All rights reserved. No part of this book may be reproduced or utilized in any form or by any means without written permission from the publisher.

Focus Readers is distributed by North Star Editions:
sales@northstareditions.com | 888-417-0195

Produced for Focus Readers by Red Line Editorial.

Content Consultant: Jacob Wiebel, PhD, Assistant Professor in African History, University of Durham

Photographs ©: Shutterstock Images, cover, 1, 4–5, 8–9, 11, 14–15, 19, 20–21, 23, 26–27, 28; Red Line Editorial, 7; AP Images, 13; iStockphoto, 16; Dominika Zarzycka/NurPhoto/AP Images, 25

Library of Congress Cataloging-in-Publication Data
Library of Congress Cataloging-in-Publication Data is available on the Library of Congress website.

ISBN
979-8-88998-221-0 (hardcover)
979-8-88998-277-7 (paperback)
979-8-88998-383-5 (ebook pdf)
979-8-88998-333-0 (hosted ebook)

Printed in the United States of America
Mankato, MN
012025

## ABOUT THE AUTHOR

Samantha S. Bell lives in the foothills of the Blue Ridge Mountains with her family and lots of cats. She is the author of more than 150 nonfiction books for kids from kindergarten through high school. She loves learning about the different countries and cultures that are part of our amazing world.

# TABLE OF CONTENTS

**CHAPTER 1**
## Welcome to Ethiopia 5

**CHAPTER 2**
## History 9

**CHAPTER 3**
## Climate, Plants, and Animals 15

**CLIMATE CRISIS IN ETHIOPIA**
## Rain Problems 18

**CHAPTER 4**
## Resources, Economy, and Government 21

**CHAPTER 5**
## People and Culture 27

Focus Questions • 30
Glossary • 31
To Learn More • 32
Index • 32

**CHAPTER 1**

# WELCOME TO ETHIOPIA

Ethiopia is a country in the eastern part of Africa. Ethiopia shares borders with several other African countries. But it does not border an ocean or a sea. The country is fully landlocked.

Ethiopia is known for its highlands. These mountains stretch on either side of the East African Rift. The country's

**Ethiopia is called the Roof of Africa because of its high mountain areas.**

highest peak is Ras Dashen. Ethiopia also has flat lowlands. **Tropical** forests cover some of its mountain areas. Other parts are grassy.

The East African Rift crosses Ethiopia. Earth's **crust** split there and spread apart. The rift is still growing today. The whole area is known as the Great Rift Valley.

Ethiopia's capital and largest city is Addis Ababa. Addis Ababa is in the highlands. It is in the center of the country. More than five million people live there. Bahir Dar is another major city. This city is in the northwest. Tourists visit for its natural beauty. They go to see the Blue Nile River and Blue Nile Falls.

Ethiopia is one of the world's oldest independent countries. It has changed a lot over its history. But across time, people have admired its land and culture.

## MAP OF ETHIOPIA

CHAPTER 2

# HISTORY

Humans have lived in Ethiopia for thousands of years. Ancient Ethiopians farmed the land. They also traded. Eventually, different groups of people came together. They formed a kingdom called Aksum.

The kingdom of Aksum was based in the highlands. Sea trade and farming

Across history, many Ethiopian farmers have passed down their land through their families.

9

helped Aksum gain power. The kingdom's rule reached across the Red Sea.

Around 340 CE, an Egyptian Christian arrived in Aksum. His name was Frumentius. He taught his religion to King Ezana. The king made Christianity the official religion. By this time, the kingdom was known as Ethiopia.

In the 600s, Muslim Arabs arrived in North Africa. Ethiopia lost control of the coasts. That weakened the kingdom. Over the 1200s and 1300s, various royal families held control. The Zagwe **dynasty** was one. The Solomonic dynasty was another. This family claimed to descend from King Solomon and the Queen of

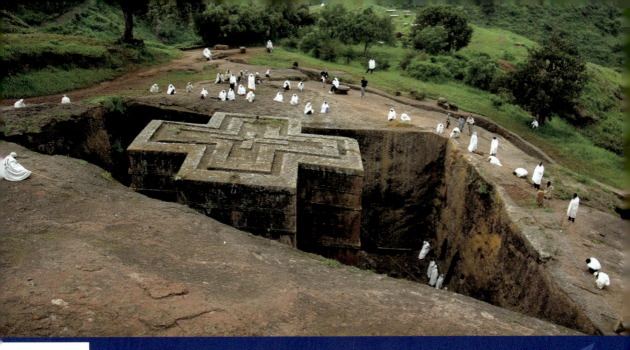

During the Zagwe dynasty, people built rock churches in the town of Lalibela.

Sheba. The claim was important to royal power for centuries.

In 1529, Muslim armies came. Ethiopia partnered with Portugal. They stopped the attack. Soon after, the Ethiopian **emperor** became Roman Catholic. But the people rejected any change in their faith. A civil war broke out.

In 1855, Tewodros II came to power. Some people call this the start of modern Ethiopia. But by the late 1800s, the country faced a new threat. European countries wanted to start **colonies** in Africa. In 1896, Italy attacked Ethiopia. But Ethiopians raised a huge army. They defeated the Italians. Ethiopia also expanded to include nearby societies.

In 1935, Italy invaded again. The emperor was forced out. Ethiopia's borders shifted even more. And in 1974, another change came. Many people were unhappy with the government. So, they overthrew it. The military took over. The military stayed in power for 17 years.

Haile Selassie ruled Ethiopia for 44 years before his removal from power in 1974.

The country's new rulers were **Communists**. They used violence against people who disagreed. During the 1980s, many Ethiopians suffered hunger. In the 1990s, a new government was formed. This government claimed to be a democracy.

**CHAPTER 3**

# CLIMATE, PLANTS, AND ANIMALS

The Ethiopian highlands have three seasons. The dry season goes from October through January. February to May is the short rainy season. The long rainy season comes next. It goes from June through September.

Ethiopia's lowlands are very warm and dry. Dallol is an area in the north. It is

**Ethiopia's rainy seasons help farmers grow crops.**

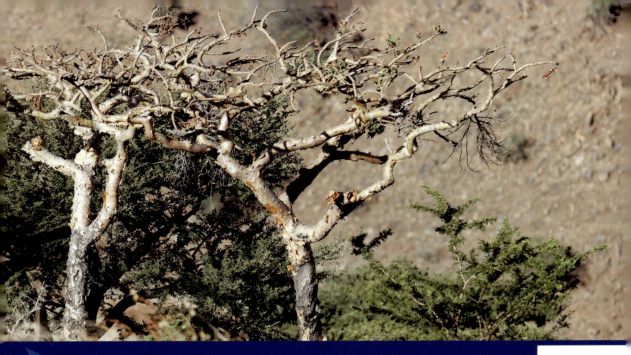

People make perfumes and medicines from some of Ethiopia's native trees.

one of the hottest places in the world. In contrast, the highlands in the center of the country are cooler. And rainforests in the southern and western areas get heavy rain.

A huge variety of wildlife lives in Ethiopia. The country has more than 800 types of birds. It also has more than

100 kinds of lizards. Some of Ethiopia's animals are rare. Rare animals include black-maned lions and gelada baboons.

Ethiopia also has a wide variety of plant life. Coffee is originally from Ethiopia. Acacia trees grow in the grasslands. In addition, Ethiopia has the only rose species native to Africa.

## BRINGING BACK THE TREES

Over time, Ethiopia lost a huge number of its trees. People burned some wood for energy. Other forest land was farmed. But without trees, the soil became dry and unusable. In 2019, the government started new projects. People planted billions of trees. And they promoted the need for healthy green spaces.

## CLIMATE CRISIS IN ETHIOPIA

# RAIN PROBLEMS

**Climate change** affects countries across the world. Often, its effects are stronger in poorer countries. These places don't have as many resources to fight the problems. That is the case in Ethiopia.

Climate change affects the country's rainy seasons. Some areas are receiving less rain than they did in the past. That causes terrible **droughts**. During droughts, people can't grow enough food. Children often get sick. In many cases, families must move. They try to find food and water elsewhere. That often means children have to drop out of school.

In other areas, climate change leads to the opposite problem. Some parts of Ethiopia receive too much rain. The heavy rain causes flooding.

Floods can happen in cities as well as rural areas.

Rushing water damages buildings and blocks roads. Electricity is cut off from houses. People may die from these events.

Climate change harms Ethiopia in other ways, too. Heat waves make people sick. And warm temperatures help diseases such as malaria spread faster.

**CHAPTER 4**

# RESOURCES, ECONOMY, AND GOVERNMENT

Ethiopia is one of the world's poorest countries. But since the early 2000s, its economy has grown very quickly. Agriculture is a big part of the economy. Ethiopia has more farm animals than any other African country. That includes more than 60 million cows and 50 million goats.

> More Ethiopians work in agriculture than in any other industry.

Many of Ethiopia's animals are **exported** to countries in the Middle East. Ethiopia also exports coffee. About half of it goes to European countries. Ethiopia exports many kinds of grain, too. They include barley and maize. All of these products come from farming.

Ethiopia creates a lot of hydroelectric power. That means water is used to

## BEE PRODUCTS

Beekeeping is a major business in Ethiopia. People in the country own millions of beehives. That helps Ethiopia make the most honey in Africa. Most of the honey is used locally. People make products such as candles. They also make tej, a honey wine.

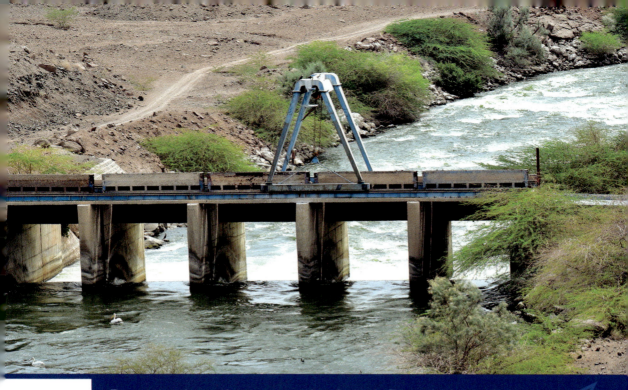

Dams such as the one on the Awash River help make electricity.

make electricity. The country also uses natural gas for energy. It has one of the largest deposits of natural gas in Africa. But people have not been able to fully use this resource. The same is true of Ethiopia's gold. Political problems make it difficult to extract these resources.

Ethiopia has three branches of government. One is the executive branch. The prime minister leads that branch. This person is the head of Ethiopia's government.

The legislative branch makes laws. It has two parts. One part is the House of Peoples' Representatives (HOPR). Ethiopians vote to choose its members. The second part is the House of Federation. Other government officials choose its members. They represent different regions and ethnic groups.

The third branch is the judicial branch. The country's courts make up this branch. Ethiopia has state and national courts.

Prime Minister Abiy Ahmed Ali speaks at a United Nations conference in 2023.

Ethiopia also has a president. The HOPR elects the president. This role does not have much power. However, the president chooses people to be in some government positions. The president also meets with officials from other countries.

CHAPTER 5

# PEOPLE AND CULTURE

Ethiopia has the second-largest population in Africa. By the early 2020s, more than 120 million people lived there. The population includes many different cultural groups. The two largest groups are the Oromo and the Amhara. Each group has its own **traditions**. For example, some have traditional dances.

> People sell items at basket markets in the city of Aksum.

Medhane Alem Cathedral is the largest church in Ethiopia.

People may do these dances to celebrate special occasions.

Many languages are spoken across Ethiopia. The country has five official languages. They include Amharic, Afaan Oromo, Afar, Tigrinya, and Somali. Many ethnic groups have their own languages or dialects. The most-spoken foreign language is English.

Religion also plays a large role in many Ethiopians' lives. A little under half the population is Christian. Most are part of the Ethiopian Orthodox Tewahedo Church. Some people are Protestants. Islam is the country's second-largest religion. Ethiopia's diverse population adds to its unique culture.

## COFFEE TIME

Coffee is part of everyday life for many Ethiopians. People may get it cheaply on the street. Some may buy expensive coffee in fancy hotels. Ethiopians may also serve the drink in a coffee ceremony. This event brings people together. It can be a way to show respect and welcome people. The oldest and most-respected guests are served first.

# FOCUS QUESTIONS

*Write your answers on a separate piece of paper.*

1. Write a paragraph explaining the main ideas of Chapter 4.

2. If you visited Ethiopia, what would you be most excited to see? Why?

3. When did Tewodros II come to power?
    - **A.** 1529
    - **B.** 1855
    - **C.** 2019

4. Ethiopia makes less money from honey than from other types of agriculture. Why might that be?
    - **A.** Ethiopia has very few beehives.
    - **B.** Most of the honey is not exported.
    - **C.** Most of the honey is not used.

*Answer key on page 32.*

# GLOSSARY

**climate change**
A human-caused global crisis involving long-term changes in Earth's temperature and weather patterns.

**colonies**
Areas controlled by a country that is far away.

**Communists**
People who support a system in which all property is owned by the public.

**crust**
The layer of rock that covers Earth.

**droughts**
Long periods of little or no rain.

**dynasty**
A series of rulers who all come from the same family.

**emperor**
A ruler who controls a group of nations or territories.

**exported**
Sent to other countries for sale.

**traditions**
Ways of doing things that are passed down over many years.

**tropical**
Having weather that is usually warm and wet.

# TO LEARN MORE

## BOOKS
Gale, Ryan. *Your Passport to Ethiopia.* North Mankato, MN: Capstone Press, 2021.
Jopp, Kelsey. *Africa.* Mendota Heights, MN: Focus Readers, 2021.
Klepeis, Alicia Z. *Ethiopia.* Minneapolis: Bellwether Media, 2023.

## NOTE TO EDUCATORS
Visit **www.focusreaders.com** to find lesson plans, activities, links, and other resources related to this title.

## INDEX

Addis Ababa, 6–7
Aksum, 9–10

Bahir Dar, 6–7
Blue Nile Falls, 6
Blue Nile River, 6–7

Christianity, 10–11, 29
climate change, 18–19
Communists, 13

Dallol, 15

East African Rift, 5–7
Ezana, 10

farming, 9, 17, 21–22
Frumentius, 10

government, 12–13, 17, 24–25
Great Rift Valley, 6

highlands, 5–7, 9, 15–16

Islam, 29
Italy, 12

languages, 28

Portugal, 11

rainy seasons, 15, 18
Ras Dashen, 6–7

Solomonic dynasty, 10–11

Tewodros II, 12

wildlife, 16–17

Zagwe dynasty, 10

Answer Key: 1. Answers will vary; 2. Answers will vary; 3. B; 4. B